Hey Dog! Sniffs are for Feet!

Hey Dog! Sniffs are for Feet!

Wendy Keefer

Illustrations by Sarah Hobbs

The Book Guild Ltd

First published in Great Britain in 2019 by
The Book Guild Ltd
9 Priory Business Park
Wistow Road, Kibworth
Leicestershire, LE8 0RX
Freephone: 0800 999 2982
www.bookguild.co.uk
Email: info@bookguild.co.uk
Twitter: @bookguild

Typeset in Minion Pro

Printed and bound in Great Britain by CPI Group (UK) Ltd, Croydon, CR0 4YY

ISBN 978 1912881 734

British Library Cataloguing in Publication Data.
A catalogue record for this book is available from the British Library.

To all the dogs I have loved before

Contents

Introduction   ix

Chapter 1   Who's Gonna Break the News to Fido?   1
             Realistic Expectations   2
             Preparing Your Dog   3
             Preparing Your Home –
             Management Tools   5
             Summary   6

Chapter 2   Goodness Me! Look What's Arrived!   7
             Do You Want Interaction?
             The Argument for 'No'   8
             But what if your answer is "Yes?"   10
             A Happy Dog = A Happy Family   11
             A Note About Photos   14
             Summary   15

Chapter 3   How Does One So Small Move So Fast?   16
             Supervision   17

	Danger Areas	19
	Copy Cat Kids	19
	Wrestling	20
	It's the Dog's Choice	21
	Side by Side Play	22
	Games for Toddlers and Dogs	22
	Toddler Games	22
	Summary	23
Chapter 4	Best Friends in the Making	24
	Understanding Dogs	25
	Never punish the growl!	28
	'Talking' Back to Your Dog	28
	Stand Still / Hands Down / Look Away / Wait	29
	Give the Dog a Choice	31
	One-Hand Touch, Two-Hands Too Much	31
	Other People's Children	32
	Teach Children They Can be Important to Dogs	33
	Summary	34
Appendix	What Was That? Training	35
References		37
About Me		38

Introduction

First of all, thank you to all you parents, grandparents, dog owners and carers of children. I am overjoyed you are reading this book!

Did you know the number of reported dog bites to people in the UK increased by 76% between 2005 and 2015? It is approximately the same in the US.

Shocking, isn't it? Perhaps more frightening is that at least 50% of those bites are to children under the age of ten.

Most of the dogs doing the biting are otherwise good, well-mannered pets in their own homes that are inadvertently pushed way beyond tolerable limits.

Take note of this: these are not stray dogs randomly biting our children, these are *our* pets. Our lovely, adorable, furry-faced pals.

So, what can we do about it?

There is a lot of great information for parents out there but most of it is either all about the child or all about the dog or let's face it, it's so boring you read the first three pages and put it aside until you've done your master's degree.

Well, my friend, Hey Dog and I sat down over beer and popcorn one night and decided we wanted to write our own book. I'll use my knowledge and experience in dog behaviour and training and Hey Dog will crop up now and then with his little friend, Gretel.

So here it is.

We've written a book that is reader-friendly and full of tips and ideas to help your kids grow up safely and happily around dogs. The book is organised into rough age groups but do read the previous chapters as much of the information is usable throughout life. Oh, and don't worry if you aren't starting in pregnancy. You can use all this stuff, the knowledge, training and management tips at any time. It just takes a bit more organisation once the baby arrives. Also, we've made sure the needs of your dog are not forgotten. After all, he's an important part of the family as well.

I should say this book is *not* a replacement for good socialisation and training for your dog and responsible parenting for your child. You will notice I emphasise supervision and I show you what that really means. I also mention giving the dog a choice repeatedly in this book. Children and dogs need to have safe, supervised and *welcome* interactions.

I strongly recommend parents, like all dog owners, refer to their local trainers and behaviourists and make use of their services. Some, like me, will offer family consultations in your home for personalised advice and guidance. Use it. It could be invaluable.

However, once you've read this book you will feel much more confident about how to keep your children safe and your dog happy.

You will understand the signals your dog is giving off and you will have a bulging toolbox of ideas to draw on to help you manage the world your children share with your dog.

Enjoy!

P.S. You will notice I refer to the child in this book as 'she' and the dog as 'he'. This is not a gender bias, it's just a bit cumbersome to use them both all the time!

Gretel   Hey

Chapter 1

Who's Gonna Break the News to Fido?

"You wont believe what's happening at my house," Barney looked glum.
"What?" asked Tootsie
"Well, today she came home from shopping with a new mattress for my crate.
It was the softest and comfiest I've ever seen."
"Really?"
"Yeah, and before that she brought in some fantastic new toys. I haven't had
any new toys for five years."
"Oh, no!" Tootsie gasped. "I know what this means. Next she'll be coming
home with a baby! Bummer, mate."

"I know. She better not think I'm sharing my bowl as well."

Congratulations!

You are expecting a baby! What an exciting time this will be for you. And big congratulations for choosing to read this book to prepare your home and your dog for a happy future together. Let us start with…

Realistic Expectations

As you are reading this book you probably already have a dog. But even if you are just thinking of getting one, you no doubt have a picture in your mind of how your dog is going to fit into your family. Whatever this picture is, it will involve change for all.

From the dog's point of view, he will need to learn that you are no longer spending the time with him that you used to. He will recognise his routine has changed and he certainly will be aware of the screaming, burping little wiggly thing you have suddenly become enamoured with.

But please remember this: dogs live very much *'in the here and now'*. They do not have the ability to plan for the future like we do. This means they are unable to aspire to world domination and they do not do things 'to get back at you'. After the baby arrives you may find the dog you thought you knew starts acting clingy or shows some unexpected behaviour. It may be he is simply not coping very well with all these changes. After all, he has no idea how much fun this baby will be when she grows up a bit.

Our aim is to make him happy in his new life and to help you to still look after his needs. Early preparation is best so read on for some tips from Hey Dog and me.

Preparing Your Dog
Early Training Tips:

- **Teaching Calmness and Settle.** You definitely will be spending lots of time with your new baby and you don't want to be getting constant nudging for attention from your dog. So practise rewarding him for simply relaxing.
- **Provide a Place of Safety.** A place of safety should be a cosy spot, for instance, in your dog's crate, where you have a household rule that your dog is never to be disturbed. Make sure your dog always has access to this place and can go there whenever he chooses. Keep it comfy and uncluttered, and don't feel tempted to spray it with disinfectants, etc. too often, as it may just put your dog off going in there. Oh, and keep the door open at all times.
- **Time Alone.** There will be times when you need your dog to be happy with a barrier between you so you can look after your baby's needs. Make this feel like a treat for your dog. Give him a nice chew or food puzzle that you save just for these occasions. If your dog isn't used to being without you, introduce him to it in short bursts at first.

  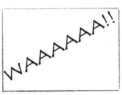

- **What Was That?** Preparing your dog for the unexpected. This is a method of training your dog to cope with the new sounds and movements the baby, and subsequent toddler/child will throw into his life. It's a simple process of desensitising him to being startled. Look at the back of the book for this method in detail. It may be the most important training you ever do with your dog.

Smells:

- Introduce your dog to the smells of a baby before the arrival if you can.
- If someone can bring a blanket the baby has been wrapped in from the hospital for your dog to smell, he will already have had an introduction to the baby before she comes home.

Sounds:

- Introduce your dog to the sounds of a baby.
- Try using downloaded sounds or a sound CD and do your 'What Was That?' training as you play them. A good tip is to get a baby-sized doll and hold it as you play the sounds.

Preparing Your Home – Management Tools

Creating a safe yet happy home is so important when dogs and children are involved. A dog, however good, should *never* be left alone with a baby or small child.

When you can't give your undivided attention, management tools are indispensable. These come in many forms:

- **Crates/Cages.** A crate is a great safe place for many dogs. If your dog isn't already crate trained make sure you introduce it slowly with the door open and plenty of good reasons to want to go in. Try using your dog's favourite chew or toys.
- **Gates.** Baby gates can be used to divide rooms as well as block off stairs. Get your dog used to being on the other side from you early on. Make it a rewarding place to be, not a punishment.
- **Room Dividers.** If you don't have a separate room for the dog or want to all be in the same one, plastic fencing can be used to give the dog his own space.
- **Puppy Play Pens.** Create a play pen for your puppy or small dog with a comfy bed and chew toys.
- **Child Play Pens.** When you are busy or want to spend time with your dog, these can be a parent's friend.
- **Dog Walker.** If you can afford to hire a dog walker or are lucky enough to have a friend or family member who can help out, get this organised ahead of time.

Practise with these management tools before the baby arrives. Walk around and sit holding a baby-sized doll. Remember to close gates and doors between the doll and the dog if you want to put it down. (You don't have to do this when other people are watching!)

"I love it when she feels guilty"

A portable tool like a play pen can also be used when visiting grandparents or friends. It can help you relax around a dog you may not know as well as your own.

Summary

So now you are armed with some ideas you can start putting them into practise.

- Have a look around your home and start using gates and crates and think about how rooms might be divided.
- Get started with training your dog to settle quietly in the room with you if he doesn't already and/or get him used to spending time happily in a different space to you.
- Importantly, start your 'What Was That?' training so the sounds and actions of the new baby become a signal of good things in your dog's mind. Continual practise also helps you train yourself to automatically say, "What Was That?" in a bright cheerful voice. Someday, you may find you use it in a potentially dangerous situation when your dog might otherwise have reacted badly.

Now, read on as we head into the world of a baby-filled home!

Chapter 2

Goodness Me! Look What's Arrived!

Millie opened her eyes and watched as the creature slowly and unsteadily got to its knees. There was a wobble and a hesitant start, then a squeal and the creature suddenly picked up speed. It was coming for the dog. Millie started to panic. She glanced from side to side. Where could she go? This was her bed, her safe place. What had happened to her quiet home?

Just then, the woman cut across the creature, deftly distracting her with a jam sandwich.

Millie sighed and settled back into her bed. "Where is my jam sandwich?" she thought as she drifted back to sleep.

So, you have prepared your dog with sounds, smells and 'What Was That?' training and you've been round the house looking for placement of child gates and dog crates. Well done. You are ready for that huge change the arrival of the baby will make in all your lives.

Now the first big decision…

Do You Want Interaction?
The Argument for 'No'

The moment the baby comes into the house your dog will probably want to investigate her. You may have been practising with a doll but the real thing is far more interesting or possibly even frightening to your dog. Is it a good idea to allow that investigation?

Then as a baby's vision develops, she rapidly becomes fascinated by everything in her environment, especially things that move. Soon, she doesn't just want to look at things she wants to touch and explore with her hands and mouth. As a parent, you will know it is important to carefully control these explorations so they are safe and happy learning experiences.

Your dog is a wondrous and mysterious creature as far as a baby is concerned. Soft and fluffy perhaps, with sparkly eyes and handles on the side of his head. Wow, what a temptation! But is now the time to encourage her to put her hands on the dog?

In making this decision there are three things to consider:

1. How does your dog feel about all this? Is he happy to have his 'handles' pulled and his 'sparkles' poked? Some dogs are more tolerant than others but they all have their limits.

2. It may turn out you have the most tolerant pup in the neighbourhood but do you want to raise a toddler that runs up to every dog in the park? Children under the age of five or six are not developmentally capable of judging the friendliness of a dog.

3. Likewise, your dog may decide he *lurves* babies. After all, they are usually covered in sticky stuff. However, his tongue may not be as welcome for some of the other parents in the park.

Your answer to the question, 'Do I allow interaction?' may be 'No' for now. That's fine.

But What If Your Answer is 'Yes?'

Many parents will feel strongly that the dog is a part of the family and they want him to get to know the baby. You may also want your child to grow up loving dogs and you are committed to teaching her to be kind and respectful from the beginning.

All of this love and respect is perfectly possible to have in a safe way if you follow a few simple rules:

- **Every interaction must be managed by an adult.** Independent approaches by the dog toward the baby or vice-versa should be discouraged in a pleasant way by using distraction or barriers. It is vital an adult is in control.
- **The dog must make the choice to approach.** He must also be able to move away at any time. Whenever a dog and a child come close to each other it must be the *dog's* decision. This is a point about bite prevention, not obedience. A dog under pressure may lash out.
- **Sniffs are for feet.** If you are holding a baby for your dog to meet, encourage sniffs to feet and legs, not heads.

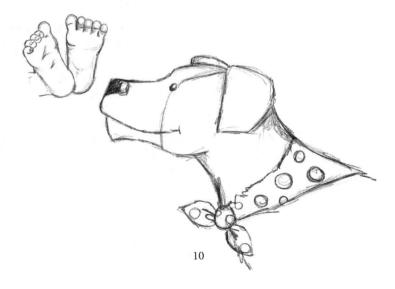

- **One-Hand Touch, Two-Hands Too Much.** This is a rule to teach from the beginning. Guide your baby's hand with yours to stroke the dog's shoulder nearest you. Allowing two hands can lead to grabbing, holding and hugging which many dogs can't cope with.

Whatever you decide about interaction you will be able to manage. Much of the time, however, your life will revolve around your new child and even with the best of intentions, your dog will have to fit into the background.

It is worth bearing in mind that…

A Happy Dog = A Happy Family

A home with a baby is a busy place: you'll be juggling housework, shopping, relationships and possibly work. The last thing you want is to throw into the mix a dog that is disruptive and destructive out of boredom. Likewise, it would be heart-breaking to find your best buddy has become depressed and withdrawn with the stress of it all. It's important the physical and emotional needs of your dog are kept fulfilled.

Here is a list of ideas, some obvious, some not so:

- **Food.** It is unlikely your dog will let you forget he needs food and water but bear in mind these need to be away from the baby as she starts to become more mobile. A quiet, toddler-free zone to feed your dog is essential.
- **Exercise.** Your life will have become full of baby essentials but this is one dog-essential that if forgotten too often, may make your life hell, and the dog's life miserable too. Get help if you can. A tired, emotionally fulfilled dog is a calmer and happier dog.
- **Sleep.** Dogs spend at least 50% of their time sleeping or dozing. This is greater for puppies and older dogs. Like us, their patience levels will be much higher if they are getting

enough sleep and enough exercise. Make sure your dog has a place he can feel safe sleeping undisturbed.

There are bound to be moments when the baby herself is asleep (yes, it will happen!) or is content in her chair or playpen. Take a few moments out from other jobs to play some games with your dog. Challenging his brain is good for his emotional health and your relationship with him. Try:

- **Trick training.** Teach him spins, down-sit-down, roll-over, touch-the-spot, the possibilities are endless and there are plenty of great resources out there if you need help or ideas.

- **What Was That?** Make use of grunts, squeals and cries from your baby to practise rewarding him for remaining calm.
- **Sit down and cuddle your dog for a minute.** Strokes and cuddles are wonderful for your emotional health as well! Remember that you'll be carrying baby's smell so cuddling will further reinforce your dog's familiarity with her.

When you want your dog happily occupied by himself, there are lots of different challenges you can give him in the form of food puzzles. Here are a few ideas:

- **Fill a cardboard box.** Use paper and cardboard food packets, throw a few treats in them and let him rip them apart.
- **Make a snuffle mat.** This is to hide food in. Have a look online for how to do this.
- **Hide things.** Very small treats can be hidden around a room before you send him in. You could even stick cheese to surfaces or hide it in small boxes to be ripped apart.
- **Commercial puzzle products.** There are loads out there. Have a look at your local pet store or online for ideas.

- **Scatter-feeding.** Throw his entire bowl of dry kibble into the garden and let him forage around to find it. Believe me, dogs love it!

A Note About Photos

Oh, my goodness, don't we all love those cute photos of dogs and babies. There is something about the vulnerability of a baby curled up against a dog that plucks at our heartstrings. We can even kid ourselves the dog is protecting this new member of his family.

However, it's important to step back and give this some thought. We can't assume that just because our dog loves us, he will instantly love our baby. As adults, we have developed a relationship with our dog that is rewarding for both parties and has rules and predictability. Even a dog that has experience with children and babies cannot be guaranteed to be happy with this one.

The reason more children under ten are bitten than any other age group is that, to a dog, a small child has no rules or predictability. They make sudden, unexpected movements and sounds. Some dogs with a high tolerance level can cope, but to many dogs this can be unsettling or even frightening. To a very few, it may even trigger a predatory response.

Consider this:

- Pose the baby/toddler in the arms of an adult or with an adult seated between the baby and dog.
- As with every other interaction, make sure the dog is there by choice.
- Try to avoid inappropriate and dangerous poses such as placing a baby or child on a dog or near a dog's face. You would not be fast enough to intervene if the dog lashed out.

Summary

I hope Chapter 2 has got you thinking about a few things, namely:

- Do you want direct interaction between your baby and your dog?
- If so, how will you manage it?

There is no need to rush your decision.

Do use caution with photographs, though. Try not to get drawn into the false sense of security the internet may offer. You don't want your child or your dog to be the one that loses out.

I also hope you have benefitted from the ideas for keeping your dog happy and your relationship with him intact.

Now we enter the chaotic world of the toddler...

Chapter 3

How Does One So Small Move So Fast?

"If you give me a lick of your bone I'll let you pull the legs off my monkey"

I remember the distant days of toddler-hood. One glance at the supermarket shelf and he or she was off, halfway down the aisle like a little rocket. Or trying to be helpful by pulling down a box of cereal, whilst simultaneously knocking another four onto the floor.

Oh yes, those were the days. Now I think the speed and impulsiveness of one so small can only be admired. However, I'm sure frustration was my overriding emotion at the time.

When it comes to the dog at home, this is where management tools like gates and barriers prove their value and supervision is paramount.

There is really only one certainty when it comes to toddlers: *The Unexpected Will Happen.*

Supervision

All this stuff you've been practising with your baby really comes into play now that you've got a toddler. Safety around dogs is so much easier with forward planning and active involvement.

Management tools should be pretty straight-forward. Gates and doors are either open or shut. Dogs and children either have access to each other or are securely separated. I'm sure you've got the gist.

But at other times you might ask yourself, "I'm in the room, but am I *actually* supervising?"

"Quick while they're not looking"

"WAAAAAA!"

The internet is a font of information and entertainment. There is no shame in admitting you may just now and then need some mental stimulation that doesn't have a small child in it.

Not only that, but today's life is so demanding. Friends, work and spouses all expect you to be instantly contactable.

The important bit is picking the right moments.

Being actively involved whenever your child and your dog are sharing the same space is very important.

You will know by now the speed in which a peaceful scenario can change. One minute you are sending an email/washing the dishes/answering the doorbell and the next minute the dog yelps and you turn to find your toddler is trying to ride Fido like a bucking bronco.

Not a happy Fido.

"In your dreams, kid"

So use your management tools. Separate your dog and toddler when you know you can't give them your full attention. If you consciously practise, this it will soon become automatic.

Being proactive about preventing a potentially dangerous situation is much less stressful than simply reacting to situations as they occur.

Danger Areas

There are certain dog-related places around your home that should always be off-limits for a toddler. These are:

- **Food Areas.** Feeding times and when the dog has a bone or treat are times a child should be kept at a safe distance. The most placid dog can be protective of his edibles. Likewise, when your child is eating. Many dogs will learn to snatch food from a child. This could lead to an accidental bite.
- **Toys.** Teach your small child she is never to take a toy from your dog's mouth and teach your dog to drop toys and back away when asked. If it's important to you that the dog gives a toy to hand, have him put it in your hand, not the child's.
- **Beds.** Beds should be places of calm and safety for a dog. If your dog wakes to find your child looming over his bed, he could feel trapped and react accordingly.
- **Anywhere** a dog could find themselves cornered by your child is a danger area.

Copy Cat Kids

Children learn by example. Every parent is amused when their two year old first picks up the television remote and points it at the TV. You know you never actively instructed her on how to use it or what it does but she learned through observation.

Remember this when you are with your dog. You may have a dog that actually loves a good cuddle with you. Dogs are social animals and many are very tactile. But the reality is that even the cuddliest of dogs will only tolerate hugs from the people they most trust. As mentioned before, trust comes from predictable, rewarding behaviour. Toddlers are anything but predictable and their behaviour is often not rewarding for the dog.

So try to restrain yourself from two-handed stroking or hugging of your dog when your small child is in sight. Instead set the **One-Hand Touch, Two-Hands Too Much** example for your youngster.

A really good idea is to get your toddler a toy dog or other such cuddly animal. Encourage her to give her strongest displays of affection to the toy instead of the dog. You can show her how to stroke and groom her toy whilst you do the real thing.

Of course, as always, remember that any parent-guided interactions your child has with your dog must be given with the dog's 'consent'. He should be called to the child and always have the option to leave.

Wrestling

Dare I say, another 'no-no' for parents and older children is wrestling or otherwise winding up your dog until he becomes over-excited. This type of play happens between puppies and young dogs as fun and a way of learning social boundaries. Boundaries are discovered when one pup bites a little too hard and the game ends.

Children should not be on the receiving end of this. They are not puppies. If your pup becomes over-aroused during play with the children, distract him with a toy and remove him from the activity for a few moments until he calms down. Ask the children to calm down, too.

It's the Dog's Choice

Running, laughing, screaming, banging and frequent falling over is pretty much the cycle of activity during the waking hours for a toddler.

Dogs almost need to be bomb-proof to survive it. Most do, but your help and attention is needed to keep a happy, if not serene household.

The place of safety you've provided for your dog will very likely be his favourite hang-out much of the time. You will probably find yourself saying 'What Was That?' (see Chapter 1) quite frequently and the treat supply will need to be replenished a lot.

However, it's also a great time to start instilling kind, respectful habits into your child when it comes to dogs. This will eventually help to create that strong bond we all like to see between our children and their pets.

As you will know, kids learn through repetition, so consistent, gentle reminders to not run at the dog, to use one hand to stroke him and most importantly, to stay with Mum or Dad and together you will call your dog rather than going to him.

As with babies, the dog must always be given a choice when it comes to approaching a young child. If he is uncomfortable about it, it's important to accept his refusal rather than be insistent he come. The better your child gets at being gentle and non-threatening to the dog, the more he will begin to see her as a positive part of his life.

Side by Side Play

A good habit to develop for your child and your dog is to encourage them to both be engaged in their own activities in the same room while ignoring each other.

For example, your dog can learn to lie calmly on his mat, perhaps with a chew or nosing a food puzzle, while your toddler is playing with her building blocks on another side of the room.

If you want to help your child develop a strong relationship with her dog, try these...

Games for Toddlers and Dogs

There are several games you and your toddler can play with your dog quite safely. These games can help your dog and your child learn how to behave around each other and, importantly, games help your dog see the small human in his life as a positive thing.

The key to playing games safely is to avoid direct contact between dog and child.

Toddler Games

- **Go Sniff!** Have your child help you hide treats or toys in the house or garden then release the dog to 'Go Sniff!' Your dog will love it!

"Stay here while I go and hide your ball"

"He he he!"

- **Find Me.**Great fun for the child, have her hide somewhere with a wooden spoon that has a smear of meat paste, peanut butter or soft cheese pressed onto it. When she is found, she can reward the dog by letting him lick this tasty treat.
- **Come and Sit.** Let your child get involved with 'training' your dog. Teach the dog that when he comes and sits a little way away, your toddler will either toss him a treat or roll one down a long tube such as a length of plumbing pipe. Great for your dog's self-control and discourages him from nibbling at your tot's hand.
- **Filling the Feeder.** Most dogs enjoy a puzzle feeder. Many of them need to have the kibble or small cubes of sausage or cheese fed into a relatively small hole. The challenge for your toddler putting them in may be just as enjoyable as the challenge of getting them out is for the dog.

Summary

Toddlers and dogs can be a real challenge, but to reduce your stress levels remember to:

- Be actively involved when they are together.
- Use reliable separation methods when necessary.

And:

- Start your child on the road to a strong relationship with 'her' dog by teaching her how to be kind and respectful from the start.

Chapter 4

Best Friends in the Making

"Mum says it's called self-control"

"Nope, never heard of it...."

Children and dogs can have such great relationships. A dog can be a playmate, companion and friend to confide in. As a parent you will want to nurture that relationship by helping your child understand their dog and become sensitive to his needs.

It is that understanding and respect that is the real key to keeping your child safe around your dog and dogs in general.

Understanding Dogs

We may ask if it is actually possible for a human to understand what a dog is trying to say and the answer is, probably not as well as another dog would. But with education, support and practise, even children can grow up to be pretty good at it. It is mostly a case of observation, as dogs primarily communicate using body language.

"Let's play charades! You first"

"Is 'Marley and Me' the only film you know?"

Understanding a dog's body language is of vital importance in reducing the risk of dog bites. Too often after a child is bitten someone is heard to exclaim, "It came out of the blue!" In reality, the dog has more than likely given lots of indications of his fear, discomfort or anger but they have not been recognised or understood by the humans around him.

Dogs, like humans, rarely escalate emotions from placid to aggressive instantly. Rather, they do their best to let us know they aren't happy, in their own doggy way. If someone doesn't respond to the dog's 'I'm unhappy' signs, their emotions could develop into full-blown aggression. Learning to recognise the early signs can be the best way to prevent aggression, and possibly a bite, from happening.

My book *Hey Dog! Let's Talk!* is the children's companion to *Sniffs are for Feet*. Part One of *Let's Talk* is illustrated with pictures of Hey Dog showing us some common dog body and facial language that says, "I'm not happy about this."

While it's important for your children to grow up knowing how to read these expressions, it's equally important for you as a parent to understand them. This will help to ensure not only the safety of your child but the comfort of your dog around your child.

Here is a list of common doggie expressions of emotion in order of increasing discomfort:

- Lip-licking, yawning, blinking or showing whites of eyes.
- Turning body away, lifting a paw, panting.
- Physically moving away.
- Standing in a slight crouch with tail tucked and ears back, pushing body weight backwards.
- Rolling onto back and showing stomach, possibly urinating.
- Stiffening and staring.

The dog may then move on to the more obvious ones:

- Growling.
- Snapping.
- Biting.

"The next time she comes at me with scissors, I'm off..."

Now, I know it's impossible to take any one of the mild expressions on their own and conclusively say a dog is anxious. Just as it's impossible to look at any snapshot in time and know for sure what someone is feeling. For example, if you look at some of those unflattering photos of celebrities the media love to publish, you have to remind yourself the camera caught only a brief moment in what was actually a continuous action.

It's the same with dogs. If you learn to recognise specific expressions of dog's sounds and body language, you can put the signs you see into the context of the bigger picture. For example, growling isn't always a warning sound, some dogs growl when they play. Watch for tension in the dog's body and face. Is it increasing or is he becoming more relaxed? Is he coming forward or leaning back?

Try observing dogs in the park interacting with other people and each other. Learn to pick up some of the common signs of discomfort and be aware of what came before and what happened next. It can be very revealing when you know what to look for.

One caution I urge every parent, though, is:

Never punish the growl!

As I said, it's very rare a dog will go from seemingly placid straight to biting. When this happens it is often because he has learned he will be punished for growling or showing his teeth.

Growling is indeed, a frightening sound to hear from a dog and our own fear instincts could cause us to lash out at him. It's important to remember this can be a dog's final warning and a bite may come next.

Instead, mentally thank him for it. Growling helps you predict your dog's behaviour. It is much safer having a predictable dog.

So, remove the child and make a note to yourself to never allow that situation to occur again. Consult your vet and/or a behaviourist if it happens more than once and especially if your dog feels a need to growl when he has ample space to move away.

'Talking' Back to Your Dog

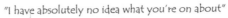

"I have absolutely no idea what you're on about"

Understanding dog body language is a big part of helping a child stay safe. The other big part is teaching the child to use her body language to tell the dog she means him no harm. You can see this illustrated in Part Two of *Hey Dog! Let's Talk!*

Dogs communicate with each other using different postures depending on the confidence of the dog and the particular circumstances in which they meet. In general, dogs aren't interested in a fight and they use non-threatening body postures to say this.

If you observe a first meeting between two dogs, you will often see the more confident dog approach and the less confident one will stand sideways and look away, allowing the initial sniff and inspection to be done. Doing this is the way the less confident dog lets the other one know they pose no threat. Even two very confident dogs rarely want confrontation. They may stand stiff and upright to each other but again, it will usually be sideways and after a cautious sniff, one or both will move slowly away, diffusing the tension. A face to face meeting is the most dangerous.

You can teach your child to mimic the non-threatening body language to let a dog know her intentions are good. For a human this is standing slightly sideways with her hands by her sides and looking away from the dog. Then she just needs to wait and see what the dog does or for help to come.

This is easy to remember by teaching your child this chant:

Stand Still / Hands Down / Look Away / Wait

This is it broken down:

- **Stand Still.** Dogs can be frightened by or attracted to movement.
- **Hands Down.** Hands by the sides is important as hands in the air can entice a dog to jump up. A child who doesn't like a dog sniffing her hands can cross her arms and tuck her hands away but remember, a very friendly dog may still want to check them for treats!
- **Look Away.** Looking just to the side or over the dog's head is fine. To a dog, looking directly into its eyes can feel like either a threat or an invitation. If your child doesn't want to meet, she can make herself boring and uninviting this way. If your child is frightened, encourage her to look at you, not at the dog.
- **Wait.** Wait to see what the dog does or, if the child is frightened by or doesn't want to interact with the dog, she can wait for help to come.

This is a great technique for many situations including:

- Meeting a new dog.
- When a child is afraid of a dog.
- To calm a boisterous dog.
- To reassure a shy dog.

If your child is ever knocked down by a playful dog, teach her to use the same 'ignoring' technique by curling up into a ball, lying still and not looking at the dog.

The tricky bit for a frightened child is remembering to stay quiet and still. Sound and movement, including crying or screaming, can be exciting to a lively dog.

Practise helps. Practise with stuffed dogs, dogs in the distance and with dogs you can trust.

(P.S. This technique also works for grown-ups!)

Give the Dog a Choice

Standing still and waiting also gives the dog the choice of approaching or not. Many dogs are shy; some are frightened of strangers and, particularly, children.

If the child wants to meet and stroke a dog I like to teach three steps:

- Stand away and ask the owner or person with the dog for permission.
- If they say yes, the child stays where they are, pats their leg and calls the dog to them. If the dog is comfortable and wants to come over, they will. If the dog chooses not to approach, the child should respect their choice and say, "That's OK, maybe another day."
- The third step is stroking the dog using One-Hand Touch.

Teaching children to stand away and call their own dog to them is always good practise. This is not to be confused with your dog having a good recall. It is about giving a dog that may be uneasy about an interaction, be it due to fear, pain or simple tiredness, permission to opt out.

One-Hand Touch, Two-Hands Too Much

Human affection is often expressed in very physical ways. We hug and kiss those we feel most love for. Most dogs too, are quite tactile. In fact, grooming, stroking and touch are an emotional requirement for dogs. It can be calming and reassuring and, as for people, it releases the hormones that produce the 'feel-good factor'. You will see many dogs enjoying physical play with their dog friends and some will even curl up together to sleep. And of course, our best doggy mates will seek physical affection from us. But they may feel differently about our children, especially when they are very young.

Humans need to trust before we are willing to share our affection. Dogs are the same. One of the best ways for a child to earn trust from a dog is to never insist on physical contact. Allow the dog to do the approaching. Speaking calmly and encouragingly and offering treats or play are all good ways to earn trust and affection.

When a dog allows contact; single-handed touching and stroking is best. The human urge to hug and kiss needs to be reined in, as many dogs find it quite frightening. Studies have shown that children are bitten in the face more than adults because they impulsively move their faces toward the things they are interested in. Instead, encourage children to stroke their dog and use words to say, "I love you." Hugs can be given to cuddly toys instead.

Teach your child to stroke the dog three or four times, pause and wait to see if the dog asks for more. This gives the dog the opportunity to say, "Thanks, I've had enough."

Other People's Children

You've worked hard to raise your kids to be considerate and respectful of dogs but can you count on other people's children to be the same? The short answer is no. Some children can be aggressive toward dogs or simply loud and unpredictable. Often, however, the hardest visitors to cope with can be the children (and parents) who have a very tolerant dog at home. They may assume all dogs will enjoy the same level of in-your-face attention because it is offered with love.

How should you deal with it?

- First of all, assume the worst is going to happen so don't be afraid to be firm and clear about *your* rules and *your* dog. You might offend someone but, hey, that's life.
- The simplest thing is to make your dog unavailable to the visitors if he is happy about being on his own. Try using gates, crates and a different room or at the least, position yourself so you can quickly intervene if a child moves toward the dog. Keep your dog on a lead if necessary.
- If you have the space and feel it's appropriate, take a positive approach and enlist the help of dog-loving children. Try saying something like, "My dog is a little scared of kids so I wonder if you would help him learn kids aren't so bad by standing over there and throwing him a few treats or his ball?"

Remember to thank them with a reminder that he isn't ready to be stroked yet, but with their help, he might be someday.

Protecting Your Dog = Protecting a Child

Teach Children They Can be Important to Dogs

The human/dog relationship has evolved over many thousands of years. Domestic dogs have changed from animals that hunt for survival into scavengers, relying on human waste, or in the developed world, into consumers of high quality manufactured foods served to them on a plate.

Our dogs also rely on their humans to fulfil most of their social needs. Thankfully, food, play and care present lots of ways

to help your child bond with her dog and teach her responsibility. As your child gets older, she can help with the care of the family pet. She can learn to feed and groom her dog, play safely and even get more deeply involved with training. Look for local classes that help to engage children with their dogs.

Summary

Dog bite prevention is a serious topic with what is often a pretty simple solution. While there are never guarantees, understanding, respect and kindness are what we can teach our children to help keep them safe. The side-effect will be happier dogs, happier kids and fewer preventable acts of aggression.

Appendix
What Was That? Training

Preparing your dog for the unexpected
The Training Process
Preparation

1. Plant small pots of easily accessible treats in each room of the house.
2. You can begin with the sounds of your own child or if you are preparing your dog for the arrival of a baby, use recorded or downloaded sounds. You'll want sounds of:

- Crying.
- Screaming.
- Laughing.
- Crashing and banging, etc.

3. If your dog is particularly sound sensitive, begin with the noise at low volume or when the baby is in another room. You can create quiet banging by dropping something deliberately onto carpet on the other side of the room from the dog.

Training

4. Create a sound loud enough to get your dog's attention but not to frighten him.
5. Immediately say, "What was that!" and give him a treat.
6. Repeat until the dog hears the noise and looks to you for a treat.
7. Perform this process until your dog can hear many different sounds at low volume and respond by looking to you for a treat.

Progression

8. Progress by introducing louder volumes and more 'real' sound – i.e. with the child in the room.
9. Gradually start dropping items nearer to the dog to mimic a child dropping or throwing a toy.
10. In training your dog, you will also be training yourself and your family to impulsively say, "What was that?" to the dog whenever something unexpected occurs.
11. Try saying it when:

- A child rides past on a bike.
- A child screams in the park.
- Your child trips over in the kitchen – especially near the dog!
- You drop a plate in the dining room.
- Etc., etc…

Don't worry about the position of your treats in the house. Having a few in your pocket at first is great but soon your dog will know your statement, "What was that?" means a treat is on its way even if you have to run into another room for it.

Use your imagination and make the unexpected a great experience for your dog.

References

Battersea Dog and Cats Home 2106, 2016. *Dog Bites: what's breed got to do with it?* [Online] Available at: https://www.battersea.org.uk/ [Accessed 20/01/2019].

Meints, K., 2017. Children and Dogs – Risks and Effective Dog Bite Prevention. In: Mills. D. and Westgarth. C, ed. *Dog Bites: A Multidisciplinary Perspective.* Sheffield: 5M Publishing Ltd., pp. 390-403.

Winter, J., 2015. *Health and Social Care Information Centre, Provisional monthly topic of interest: admissions caused by dogs and other mammals.* [Online] Available at: https://webarchive. nationalarchives.gov.uk/20180328130852tf_/http://content.digital. nhs.uk/catalogue/PUB17615/prov-mont-hes-admi-outp-ae-April%202014%20to%20February%202015-toi-rep.pdf/ [Accessed 29/01/2019].

About Me

Like all of you, I have had a multi-faceted life in one way or another. I grew up with the Rocky Mountains to explore within steps from my country home in Colorado. There I nurtured a love of animals wild and domestic, tiny and huge. I rode horses and collected bones and insects, always accompanied by a dog or two. I fantasised about being a vet or a writer of poetry but became neither.

Somehow along the way I found myself living in a one-room cabin in Alaska with a husband, two small children and my once-in-a-lifetime dog, Apple. She was an incredibly smart Border Collie that a stranger had brought into my place of work at probably, no more than six or seven weeks old. She would have been five years old when the children started arriving and she wasn't impressed. I can say with assurance, she positively disliked babies. Looking back at my naivety, I am pleased to say the children never got bitten. I guess I knew instinctively that the dog needed enough space to move away and I must have deflected the attentions of the toddlers deftly enough to prevent conflict. More luck than design, I'm sure.

But that was many long years ago. Now in England, my children are adults, my dogs are Labradors and I am changing from a career in physiotherapy to pet behaviour and training (and writing, it seems!). I have a deep concern about the growing number of dog bites and their consequences, both to child and dog, so I have set out to reach as many families as I can. I hope this book will make a difference.

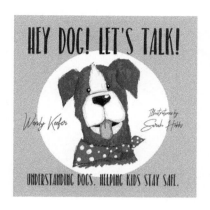

Also by the author

HEY DOG! LET'S TALK!

Hey Dog! Let's Talk! is a beautifully illustrated children's guide to understanding dogs and learning to communicate with them in a way they will understand. Written with ages four to seven in mind it is intended to be read with parents to stimulate discussion. It is the author's hope that parents will encourage their children to practise the communication techniques with the dogs around them and that this in turn will help to reduce the number of avoidable dog bites that are sadly on the increase.

The knowledge gained from this book is not only important for children wishing to develop safe relationships with their family dogs, but it can be invaluable to those who are frightened or otherwise don't want to interact with dogs at all.